THE FIRE AND THE ROSE

A RETREAT GUIDE ON THE IMMACULATE HEART OF MARY

FR. JOHN BARTUNEK, LC, STHD

Printed in the United States of America

Cover and interior design by Coronation Media

ISBN: 9798650617532

INTRODUCTION

In 1942 the forces of totalitarianism were advancing throughout the globe, bringing tyranny and terror to previously free nations and spreading death and destruction on a hitherto unimaginable scale.

Venerable Pope Pius XII, though lacking an army or a navy to contribute to the struggle of World War II, was actively committed to restoring peace. Publicly, his radio addresses crossed all borders, broadcasting a true Christian vision for the future, giving hope and encouragement to millions. He was hailed by The New York Times as "a lonely voice crying out of the silence of a continent." Privately and secretly, he was orchestrating the rescue of more than 800,000 Jews from the voracious ovens of Nazi concentration camps, even while he knew that the Catholic Church itself was also high on the list of Nazi targets.

And yet, some scholars believe that Pope Pius XII's most significant contribution was his consecration of the entire world to the Immaculate Heart of Mary, on October 31 of that same year, 1942, the twenty-fifth anniversary of the apparitions of Our Lady of Fatima. Why would such an action be considered so important? What is the real meaning behind devotion to the Immaculate Heart of Mary, for ourselves and for our world? That is what this Retreat Guide, The Fire and the Rose, will explore:

o   The Meditations will delve into the symbols contained in the image of the Immaculate Heart of Mary, and how they relate to the liturgical texts of the feast.

○ The Conference will get practical by reflecting on the four types of purity that can help us follow Mary's example in our own journey to spiritual maturity.

Let's begin by quietly turning our attention to God, who never stops paying attention to us. Let's ask him for all the graces we need, and most especially for the grace to be inspired and instructed by Mary's Immaculate Heart, which the whole Church celebrates every year on the Saturday after the Feast of the Sacred Heart of Jesus.

NOTES

FIRST MEDITATION
Two Gifts in One

INTRODUCTION

When St. Paul VI reassigned the feast of the Immaculate Heart of Mary so that every year it would immediately follow the feast of the Sacred Heart of Jesus, he did so for a reason. He wanted to make clear the connection between these two devotions.

In an another Retreat Guide, we have explored how the Holy Spirit raised up devotion to the Sacred Heart of Jesus as a way to refresh the world's understanding of God's love towards us—a personal, passionate love filled with determination, yearning, and even sorrow at our reluctance to accept it. The Sacred Heart of Jesus is an eloquent, powerful image of that love for all of us, saints and sinners alike.

JESUS GIVES US HIS MOTHER

When Jesus gave the Church the gift of his Mother while he was dying on the Cross, that too was an expression of his love, his wisdom, and his power. Just as Eve had been the one mother of the fallen human race, Jesus wanted to give us Mary as the one mother of the redeemed human race: our mother in the order of grace, as the Catechism puts it.

Through this gift we can all find in Mary an expression of the closeness and tenderness of God's love for us, a love as fierce and unconditional as the love that pours forth from a mother's heart as she nurses her helpless baby. Mary's ongoing presence in the Church speaks to us of God's own unconditional acceptance of us as his beloved children. This is one dimension behind the Church's devotion to the Immaculate Heart of Mary, the symbol of her incomparable motherly love.

And yet, throughout the history of this devotion, which really began to gather momentum in the Middle Ages at the same time that devotion to the Sacred Heart of Jesus began to gather momentum, that dimension hasn't been the primary one. Rather, the primary dimension of devotion to the Immaculate Heart of Mary has been Mary's heart as an example for our hearts, as the human heart that has loved God most purely and most perfectly. Her love is exemplary because her heart is immaculate, unhindered and unwounded by original or personal sin.

In a sense, the Sacred Heart of Jesus reveals how wonderfully God loves us, and the Immaculate Heart of Mary reveals how we are called to love him in return.

Of course, as our spiritual mother Mary not only shows us how to love God through her example, but she also helps us grow in that love through her intercession.

On the solemnity of the Sacred Heart of Jesus, then, we welcome once again the burning love that God has for us, and we worship him, filled with wonder and awe that God could care so much about us. And then, on the memorial of the Immaculate Heart of Mary, we contemplate the beauty of Mary's response to that love, a contemplation that inspires us to learn from her and follow in her footsteps.

A FOURFOLD SYMBOLISM

The traditional symbols present in artistic renditions of Mary's Immaculate Heart are the doorway through which we can discover that beauty and rekindle that inspiration.

That symbolism highlights the four especially grace-filled characteristics of Mary's heart summarized in the preface for the Eucharistic Prayer used in the liturgy on the memorial of the Immaculate Heart of Mary:

(1)…For you gave the Blessed Virgin Mary a wise and obedient heart, that she might perfectly carry out your will,

(2) a new and gentle heart, in which you were well pleased and on which you inscribed the law of the New Covenant.

(3) You gave her an undivided and pure heart, that she might be worthy to be the Virgin Mother of your Son and to rejoice to see you for ever.

(4) You gave her a steadfast and watchful heart, so that she could endure without fear the sword of sorrow and await in faith the Resurrection of her Son.

Later, we will go through these four characteristics one by one, connecting them to the symbolism of the Immaculate Heart imagery, unpacking their meaning, and being enriched by their instruction.

MARY'S IMMACULATE HEART: A GIFT FROM GOD TO THE WORLD

First, however, notice how the preface begins by reminding us that Mary's Immaculate Heart was a gift from God. The prayer begins by addressing God with the phrase, "For you gave the Blessed Virgin Mary…"

The Immaculate Heart of Mary is unique among human hearts, because from the moment of her conception

God preserved her from the effects of original sin. Here we see the connection between the dogma of Mary's Immaculate Conception and the devotion to Mary's Immaculate Heart.

A PARISIAN APPEARANCE

This connection came out vividly during Mary's apparition in 1830 to St. Catherine Labouré, a Sister of Charity living in Paris, France.

One night during vespers, Mary appeared to St. Catherine standing on a globe, framed in an oval of light, with her arms spread and her hands extended towards the globe. She wore on her fingers rings set with bright gems. From these rings rays of light streamed down to the globe. As St. Catherine described it, Mary was as radiant as a sunrise in all her perfect beauty.

Around the margin of the oval frame was written a simple prayer: "O Mary, conceived without sin, pray for us who have recourse to you." The image then rotated, and St. Catherine beheld an oval of twelve stars surrounding three images: on top, a large letter "M" surmounted by a cross, and underneath the Sacred Heart of Jesus surrounded by a crown of thorns, and right next to it the Immaculate Heart of Mary pierced by a sword.

The Blessed Virgin asked St. Catherine Labouré to have a medal created whose two sides reproduced what she had seen in the vision. Eventually, this led to the production and ecclesiastical approval of the Medal of Our Lady of Graces, better known as the Miraculous Medal.

In this wondrous apparition, then, Mary herself pairs her Immaculate Heart with the Sacred Heart of Jesus, and emphasizes that the special characteristics of her heart flow from her special privilege of being conceived immaculately, without the effects of original sin. In other words, her Immaculate Heart is more than a quaint but irrelevant expression of Catholic piety; it is as much God's wise gift to us and to the Church as is her Immaculate Conception.

In the next Meditation, we will unwrap that gift by looking at how the symbols of the image reflect the four characteristics mentioned in the preface. But for now, let's take some time, in the quiet of our hearts, to prayerfully reflect on how the Blessed Virgin Mary is a revelation both of God's tender love for us, and also of the abundant life God wants us all to experience as we follow the example and lean on the intercession of the Immaculate Heart of Mary.

QUESTIONS FOR PERSONAL REFLECTION/GROUP DISCUSSION

1. Up to this point in my life, what role has devotion to the Immaculate Heart of Mary played in my Christian journey? Why?

2. Who most naturally comes to mind when I think about an inspiring example of loving God? What is it about that person that inspires me and why?

3. How deeply have I thought about why God wants to give me the gift of Mary, as my mother in the order of grace, as an example to follow and as a powerful intercessor? How have I received this gift up to now in my life?

THREE QUOTATIONS TO AID YOUR MEDITATION

Let us look to Mary, whose discreet and holy life is a model of deep unity between interior and exterior efforts. Even in the most complex and painful circumstances, she gave the example of a life totally in harmony and trustingly abandoned herself to God's will. May the Virgin, Mirror of Perfection, obtain for every believer the courage and hope that are indispensable for setting off resolutely on a path of conversion.

—Angelus, March 3, 1996
ST. JOHN PAUL II

Dear friends, devotion to Our Lady is an important element in our spiritual lives. In our prayer, let us not neglect to turn trustfully to her. Mary will not neglect to intercede for us next to her Son. In looking to her, let us imitate her faith, her complete availability to God's plan of love, her generous welcoming of Jesus. Let us learn to live by Mary. Mary is the Queen of Heaven who is close to God, but she is also the Mother who is close to each one of us, who loves us and who listens to our voice.

—General Audience, August 22, 2012
POPE BENEDICT XVI

In the heart of the Church, Mary shines forth. She is the supreme model for a youthful Church that seeks to follow Christ with enthusiasm and docility… Today, Mary is the Mother who watches over us, her children, on our journey through life, often weary

and in need, anxious that the light of hope not fail.
For that is our desire: that the light of hope never
fail. Mary our Mother looks to this pilgrim people: a
youthful people whom she loves, and who seek her
in the silence of their hearts amid all the noise, the
chatter and the distractions of the journey. Under
the gaze of our Mother, there is room only for the
silence of hope. Thus Mary illumines anew our youth.

—*Christus Vivit*, 43 & 48

POPE FRANCIS

NOTES

SECOND MEDITATION

A Heart Full of Grace

INTRODUCTION

God gave the Blessed Virgin Mary an Immaculate Heart, and she faithfully cared for and followed that heart, and so became an example for all of us who want to grow in our love for God. Let's contemplate that heart and learn from that example.

A WISE AND OBEDIENT HEART

The first facet of Mary's heart that the liturgy highlights for us is that God gave her a "wise and obedient heart, that she might perfectly carry out his will."

Who doesn't want to be wise? Wisdom is a universal value, a universal desire. Every person longs to be wise. Every culture has produced artists, philosophers, and mystics who spent their lives searching for true wisdom.

In Mary, God himself reveals to us what true wisdom looks like: A wise heart is an obedient heart, a heart that seeks to discover and carry out God's own will. This is why Mary's Immaculate Heart is shown burning with the same fire bursting forth from the Sacred Heart of Jesus: they want the same thing; they are in perfect communion and share the same love.

In a sense, true wisdom is the same thing as lasting happiness. We can't imagine anyone being truly, deeply happy who is not also truly, deeply wise. And we can't imagine anyone who is truly wise being deeply unhappy. Jesus himself makes this connection in a conversation with one of his disciples about his Mother. This conversation is one of the Gospel passages used in the liturgy to celebrate the Immaculate Heart of Mary:

❝While Jesus was speaking, a woman from the crowd called out and said to him, "Blessed is the womb that carried you and the breasts at which you nursed." He replied, "Rather, blessed are those who hear the word of God and observe it."

—Luke 11:27–28

To hear God's word and observe it, to search for what God wants, for how God sees things, and to adjust one's own attitudes, behaviors, and choices accordingly: that is true wisdom. And that is what will lead us to becoming blessed, which is the Bible's word for the true, lasting happiness that begins in this life and flourishes for all eternity in the life to come.

A NEW AND GENTLE HEART

The liturgy identifies a second facet of Mary's heart, that it is "new and gentle," a heart in which God was "well pleased" and on which he "inscribed the law of the New Covenant."

This reminds us of what Jesus himself said about his own heart:

❝Take my yoke upon you and learn from me, for I am gentle and humble of heart, and you will find rest for your souls.

—Matthew 11:29

Among the Rabbis at the time of Jesus, the divine law - the Old Covenant - was often compared to a yoke that we put on in order for God to guide us to a fruitful life. And yet, the prophets had predicted that when God established his New Covenant, it would not just be an exterior law that was obeyed mechanically, but an interior law that would transform our very souls. Here is how Ezekiel put it:

> I will sprinkle clean water upon you, and you shall be clean from all your uncleannesses, and from all your idols I will cleanse you. A new heart I will give you, and a new spirit I will put within you; and I will take out of your flesh the heart of stone and give you a heart of flesh. And I will put my spirit within you, and cause you to walk in my statutes and be careful to observe my ordinances.
>
> —Ezekiel 36:25–37

This newness of life and freshness of heart promised to come with the New Covenant was first present in Mary, who had been preserved from the effects of original sin.

In most traditional images, at least some of the roses shown circling Mary's Immaculate heart are white, symbolizing this newness, this freshness, this gentleness and humility, which is at the same time sweet and strong. Likewise, when we follow Christ and receive his grace, our hearts become true gardens of virtue. Taking up his yoke truly does lead to rest for our souls.

AN UNDIVIDED AND PURE HEART

The third characteristic the liturgy presents to us is Mary's "undivided and pure heart," given to her so that she "might be worthy to be the Virgin Mother" of God's Son and "to rejoice to see" God forever.

Many symbols in Christian art evoke Mary's sacred, consecrated virginity, her generous and completely counter-cultural dedication to the Lord, which enabled her to become the Mother of God: a sealed fountain, the lily of the valley, the rose of Sharon, and an enclosed garden are some of those symbols. Those images all are visually echoed by the circle of roses surrounding her Immaculate Heart. Just as a garden well tended produces beautiful plants, so Mary's heart, preserved by God from original sin, became - almost literally - the soil from which Jesus himself grew and entered the world.

But her undivided love didn't end once Jesus was born. Her heart continued to be a place of fertile contemplation yielding abundant spiritual harvests throughout her life. Just like the blossoming roses encircling her heart, Mary was constantly opening herself to receive God's words and grace. More than once St. Luke alludes to this prayerful spirit, this rich interior life and spiritual sensitivity so characteristic of an undivided heart. After the shepherds' visit to Bethlehem on Christmas night, for example, he tells us:

> All who heard it were amazed by what had been told them by the shepherds. And Mary kept all these things, reflecting on them in her heart.
>
> —Luke 2:18-19

A STEADFAST AND WATCHFUL HEART

Finally, the liturgy tells us that God gave Mary a "steadfast and watchful heart, so that she could endure without fear the sword of sorrow and await in faith the Resurrection of her Son."

When Mary and Joseph first brought Jesus into the Temple, the prophet Simeon foretold that a sword would pierce Mary's heart. Most artistic renditions of the Immaculate Heart of Mary depict a single sword piercing her heart, in fulfillment of this prophecy. Some images show seven swords piercing her heart, a reference to the seven sorrows commemorated on the feast of Our Lady of Sorrows. In some images, a few of the roses surrounding her heart are red—the symbol of martyrdom in Christian art. Mary's sorrows in the face of her Son's passion and death were so deep, because she loved so fully, that she is also invoked as Queen of Martyrs.

Mary persevered in her faith and her obedience even as the sword of sorrow pierced her heart. This can be a great comfort for us, because we too experience deep sorrows as we make our pilgrimage through this fallen world. Knowing that Mary wasn't exempt from the suffering we inevitably experience, knowing that in fact her Immaculate Heart was even more sensitive than our less pure hearts, can inspire us. Her steadfast and watchful heart can be a guide and a teacher for our weak and distracted hearts.

A HEART CLOSE TO OUR HEARTS

When Mary appeared at Fatima in 1917, she showed her heart to the shepherd children, but instead of a sword piercing it, a ring of thorns surrounded it. Even so, it was still burning with love. And perhaps that is one of the reasons Venerable Pope Pius XII decided to accept Our Lady of Fatima's invitation and consecrate the whole world to her Immaculate Heart right in the middle of World War II. Not everyone, perhaps, can be inspired by Mary's purity and wisdom, because they feel so far away from being pure and wise. But we can all relate to a heart burning with love - or with the desire to love - while all it seems to encounter on its journey through the world is contradiction and opposition.

Much more could be said about the Immaculate Heart of Mary, but for now, before moving onto the conference about the four kinds of purity essential to every Christian's development, let's take some time, in the quiet of our hearts, to contemplate and be inspired by the wisdom, the gentleness, the purity, and the watchful courage of the Immaculate Heart of Mary.

QUESTIONS FOR PERSONAL REFLECTION/GROUP DISCUSSION

1. Where do I seek wisdom? What role does obedience play in my life?

2. How is Jesus encouraging me to learn how to be gentle and humble of heart, like him, in this current season of my spiritual journey?

3. In what ways is the Holy Spirit inviting me to follow Mary's example of a "steadfast and watchful heart"? How often do I ask Mary herself to be my teacher and guide?

THREE QUOTATIONS TO AID YOUR MEDITATION

❝ Mary's presence beside the cross indicates her commitment of total sharing in her Son's redemptive sacrifice. Mary had willed to participate to the very depth in the sufferings of Jesus because she did not reject the sword foretold to her by Simeon. instead, she accepted with Christ the mysterious plan of the Father. She was the first to partake in that sacrifice, and she would forever remain the perfect model of all those who would agree to associate themselves unreservedly with the redemptive offering.

—General Audience, November 23, 1988
ST. JOHN PAUL II

Queen of the Holy Rosary,
Help of the Christians,
Refuge of the human race,
Conqueress in God's battlefields,
To You and to Your Immaculate Heart
In this tragic hour of human history
We entrust and consecrate ourselves,
And the Holy Church.
She is the Mystical Body of Your Jesus,
Suffering and bleeding in so many parts
And tormented in so many ways,
We consecrate to You the whole world torn by
    bitter strife
And consumed by the fire of hatred
The victim of its own wickedness.
Look with compassion to all material and
    moral destruction
To the suffering and fears of fathers and mothers
Of husbands and wives, of brother and sisters
and innocent children.
Look at the many lives cut down in the flower of youth

So many bodies torn to pieces in brutal slaughter
So many souls tortured and troubled
And in danger of being lost eternally.
Oh, Mother of Mercy, obtain peace for us from God!
Obtain especially those graces, which can
convert human hearts quickly.
Those graces, which can prepare, establish and
        insure peace.
Queen of Peace, pray for us;
Give the world at war the peace for which all
        are longing,
Peace in Truth, Justice and the Charity of Christ.
Give them peace of the arms and peace of mind,
That in tranquillity and order
The Kingdom of God may expand.
Grant Your protection to infidels
And to those still walking in the shadow of death;
Give them peace and permit that the sun of truth
may raise upon them;
And that together with us
They may repeat before the Only Saviour of the World:
        Glory to God in the highest
        And peace on earth among men of good will
        (Luke 2:14)
Give peace to the people separated by error
        and schism,
Particularly those, who have special devotion to You
And among whom there was no home,
Where Your venerable Icon was not honoured,
Though at present it may be hidden
In the hope for better days.
Bring them back to the One Fold of Christ,

Under the One True Shepherd.
Obtain peace and complete liberty for the Holy
Church of God,
Check the spreading flood of neo-paganism,
Arouse within the faithful love of purity
The practice of Christian life and apostolic zeal,
So that the people who serve God,
May increase in merit and number.
All of humanity were once consecrated to the
Heart of Your Son.
All our hopes rest in Him, Who is in all times
Sign and pledge of victory and salvation.
Forever we consecrate ourselves to You
And to Your Immaculate Heart,
Oh, Mother and Queen of the World!
May Your love and patronage hasten the victory
of the Kingdom of God,
May all nations, at peace with each other and
with God, proclaim You Blessed
And sing with You from one end of the earth to
     the other,
The eternal Magnificat of glory, love and gratitude
To the Heart of Jesus, in which alone,
They can find Truth, Life and Peace.

—Prayer of Consecration of the World to the
Immaculate Heart of Mary, October 31, 1942
VENERABLE POPE PIUS XII

NOTES

CONFERENCE

*Fourfold Purity as a Path
of Spiritual Growth*

INTRODUCTION

Mary's unique spiritual beauty is linked to her unique privilege of being conceived without sin, of having an immaculate heart. But we were not conceived without sin. We do not have an immaculate heart. For us, growing in holiness also means cooperating with God as he heals us from the wounds of original sin and our own sins, as he purifies us in four fundamental ways.

When we hear the word "purity," we tend to think primarily of the virtue of chastity, of keeping ourselves pure of sexual sin. And yet, Catholic spiritual writers throughout the centuries have shown a much broader and more robust understanding of purity than simply equating it with chastity. In fact, understanding the four types of purity that our spiritual tradition presents to us can be a powerful tool for spiritual growth. In this conference, we will explain each of the four types of purity, and offer some practical tips on how to develop each of them. The personal questionnaire at the end of the conference will help you apply this general Xray of Christian purity to your own personal situation.

PURITY OF CONSCIENCE

Purity of conscience touches on basic morality. We keep our conscience pure by obeying the Ten Commandments and repenting as soon as we realize we have once again committed an immoral act like lying, stealing, getting drunk, gossiping, or purposely skipping Sunday Mass because of laziness.

Usually this is an important area of conscious work in the beginnings of our spiritual journey. When we have a powerful experience of God's love and goodness, the first thing we feel moved to do is repent from habits of sin that have taken root in our lives. Our conscience identifies these habits and moves us to root them out—like uprooting overgrown weeds in order to be able to plant a healthy garden.

Cultivating purity of conscience involves forming our conscience, listening to it, and obeying it. Conscience, understood at its most basic level, is the capacity of the human mind to recognize the difference between morally good and morally evil actions. Squirrels and spiders don't have a conscience, because they are not endowed with spiritual freedom. They live purely by instinct. Human beings, on the other hand, have been created in God's image, with self-awareness and the capacity of self-determination. Our conscience is the capacity God has given us to direct the use of that freedom, avoiding what is morally evil and thus spiritually destructive, and pursuing what is morally good and thus spiritually fruitful. It points out the direction of healthy moral living, and it even pushes us in that direction and approves or disapproves of our moral decisions after we make them.

CULTIVATING PURITY OF CONSCIENCE

The first step in cultivating purity of conscience is forming our conscience. This is necessary because conscience is linked to our intellect, which was darkened and damaged by original sin. We have to open it up to God's grace and truth in order to heal and strengthen it. Remember, conscience doesn't create moral good and evil, rather it recognizes moral good and evil, and informs us about the morality of the choices we make.

A good way to form our conscience is to do a guided self-examination on the Ten Commandments. This can even be done in the context of preparing a general confession, a confession of the sins of our whole life. Many guides for this kind of examination of conscience are available. They help us reflect personally on the basic moral truths revealed to us in the Ten Commandments, enlightening our conscience so as to be a trustworthy moral guide.

Once we have made a thorough self-examination, we can keep forming our conscience by continuing to study Church teaching on moral issues, and making a firm commitment to listen to and obey our conscience as it attempts to guide us in our daily life.

Most of the time, our moral choices are simple and clear. Every once in a while, however, we face a real moral dilemma. That can be an opportunity for growth by seeking out guidance from well-formed confessors or wise mentors.

PURITY OF HEART

Purity of heart has to do with our desires and affections. What do I desire? What am I attached to? What do I want? What do I think will make me happy? Our deep desires and convictions give a fundamental direction to our lives, and if they are out of synch with God's own design for our happiness, they can lead us far away from the fulfillment we yearn for.

In the end, only God satisfies our hearts. So, growing in purity of heart means growing in our desire for communion with God. It means desiring other things only insofar as they actually contribute to that communion, either because they are gifts from God for our good, or opportunities for us to glorify God by knowing, loving, and following him more fully. When our hearts reach out to things or clings to things apart from their proper relationship to God, those things become little idols that can inhibit the growth of our friendship with God.

Anything can become an idol if we get overly attached to it, if we think it will fulfill us in a way that only God can. For example, success at work is a good thing, but when we pursue it so energetically that we stop going to Mass or neglect our family responsibilities, it becomes an obstacle to our spiritual growth.

As we grow spiritually, God starts to purify our hearts in surprising ways. He knows our hearts better than we do. He knows that we often desire his gifts—like feelings of consolation in prayer, or the feelings of delight we experience when someone expresses his or her love for us—more than himself, even without being aware of it. And so he takes us through seasons of purification during which he withdraws some of his gifts, so that we can learn to desire him more purely and deeply. These types of seasons have various names among spiritual writers, names like the dark night of the soul, or dryness in prayer, or passive purification.

PURIFYING OUR HEARTS

The ongoing purification of our hearts, therefore, takes a lifetime. Our role in contributing to this purification consists primarily of conscious, faith-filled obedience to

God's will. Gradually, God's will—as mundane or costly as it may be—has to become our one desire, our one delight, our one source of contentment. This doesn't just mean doing God's will. It also means accepting and embracing God's will—after all, God's will includes all the desires he has for us, all the good that he wants for us, and all he permits to happen in our lives.

Another spiritual discipline that can contribute to the purification of our hearts is prayerful reflection on our experiences of sorrow, frustration, and worry. Often, when we encounter those kinds of interior disturbances, it is indicating some kind of subconscious fear or attachment constricting our freedom and dimming our faith. Taking time to prayerfully reflect on the real roots of why certain things that upset us can help open our hearts more fully to God's grace and discover where we need healing and purification.

PURITY OF MIND

The mind, the intellect, is the window through which we see and understand all things—the world, ourselves, and God. And so, the thoughts occupying our conscious and subconscious mind have an enormous effect on everything we do and feel. The devil knows this, and tries to take advantage of our wounded human nature by sowing lies deep within our minds—especially lies about ourselves and about how God sees us. It's no coincidence that Jesus called the devil the "father of lies" (John 8:44).

Purifying our minds involves developing mental discipline about which thoughts we pay attention to. The deeper truths that God has revealed to us in Christ gradually become the habitual landscape of our thinking as God purifies our minds. These are truths like God's absolutely reliable love, his faithfulness, his promise of heaven, the value of all our actions united to him in grace, his constant presence, the gift behind every particle of existence, and the value of God's will no matter how small it seems.

As these truths penetrate our minds more and more deeply, and as our conviction about them becomes more and more existential and personal, our minds become free from lies and distractions. This gradually enables us to experience some level of spiritual contentment even in the midst of pain and darkness. In fact, sometimes the reason God permits us to experience pain and darkness is precisely so that we can have a better chance of learning to live more fully from the deeper truths. That's when we begin to experience what St. Paul called "the peace of God that surpasses all understanding" (Philippians 4:7).

PURIFYING OUR MINDS

The best way we can contribute to purifying our minds, besides the bread-and-butter Christian disciplines of mental prayer and spiritual reading, is through practicing the discipline of silence.

The discipline of silence helps us filter out our secularized culture's unending avalanche of digital noise. The noise of today's popular culture is like a constant barbarian invasion of our minds—flooding us with thousands of images, ideas, and promises every day and all day. And very little of that noise resounds with the deeper truths. If we don't filter it out, the deeper truths will never have a chance to grow and become the real landscape of our minds.

The discipline of silence includes taking time just to be with ourselves, to be present to ourselves. It means taking time to be alone with God. And it means mastering our phones, tablets, and computers, rather than being mastered by them. Without growing in this area, we will never actually learn to decide what we think about, and our minds will constantly be polluted by the lies and seductive distractions of this fallen world.

PURITY OF INTENTION

The fourth type of purity has to do with our motivations, with why we do what we do. Purity of intention means that whatever we do, we do it motivated by faith-filled, humble love for God and his Kingdom. Gradually, as we grow in our friendship with God, all other motivations fall away. This leads us to experience interior freedom and the kind of joy that Jesus spoke of during the Last Supper; "I have told you this so that my joy may be in you and your joy may be complete" (John 15:9–11).

Here we see how all four types of purity are connected. An impure intention in our actions can be linked to a crippled conscience, an impure desire of the heart, or even a distorted mental pattern. Sometimes this link is conscious, but other times we are not fully aware of it. In our spiritual journey, God at times allows us to reach the very end of our strength in order to expose and purify our hidden motives so that we can live more fully from love and for love.

EXERCISING PURITY OF INTENTION

We can exercise purity of intention in the midst of our busy days by pausing to remind ourselves of the reasons behind what we are doing, and even offering our different activities and duties to the Lord as acts of worship. This too takes practice, and discipline. It can feel easier to switch on a kind of autopilot mentality and rush through life keeping busy, busy, busy, instead of pausing to reflect on the eternal value of what we do when we really do it out of love.

ONE FOURFOLD PATH

As we go through the choices and decisions of everyday life, these four aspects of the human spirit—conscience, heart, mind, and intention—all work together. But thinking about them individually can help us understand ourselves better, and maybe even show us where we need to grow. And in the end that's what we really want, to keep growing in our relationship with God, so that we can become more faithful children of our heavenly Father, and more faithful followers of our Lord and Savior Jesus Christ, just like the Blessed Virgin Mary.

Take some time now to prayerfully reflect on the personal questionnaire, which is designed to help you apply these general truths to your particular circumstances.

PERSONAL QUESTIONNAIRE

1. When I think of the word "purity," what associations usually come to mind?

2. How well formed is my conscience? Could I explain to a non-Christian the Ten Commandments and all their practical implications?

3. Are there any moral teachings of the Church that I don't agree with or that I don't understand? What have I done to try to understand them more deeply?

4. How often do I go to Confession? What do I do to prepare myself to make a good confession?

5. In the depths of my heart, what do I desire most? How do those desires affect my daily life?

6. How often do I take time to reflect on the direction of my life, the meaning of my life, the deepest desires of my heart? Would it be helpful for me to make a mission statement for my life?

7. What kinds of little "idols" have I had to struggle with in my life up to now? What have I learned from the struggles?

8. What do I think about most of the time? How aware am I of the thoughts that constantly flow through my mind?

9. How much does the noise of popular culture dominate the landscape of my mind? What do I do to create oases of silence and calm reflection in my day, my week, my month, my year?

10. How often do I reflect on what is motivating me in my daily activities?

11. When I find myself getting upset about something, how do I usually react? What can I do this week to

start forming the habit of prayerful reflection on what happens in my soul when I am getting upset, in order to uncover the hidden causes of that turbulence and so contribute to the purification of my conscience, heart, mind, and intention?

NOTES

FURTHER READING

St. John Paul II's Catechesis on Mary, Mother of God
(available online here: http://totus2us.com/teaching/jpii-
catechesis-on-mary-mother-of-god/)

The World's First Love
by Fulton J Sheen

Beginnings in the Spiritual Life
by Dominic Hoffman, O.P.

National Catholic Register's Confession Guide for Adults
(available online here: http://www.ncregister.com/info/
confession_guide_for_adults)

*Noise: How Our Media-saturated Culture Dominates
Lives and Dismantles Families*
by Teresa Tomeo

The Power of Silence
by Robert Cardinal Sarah

EXPLORING MORE

Please visit our website, *RCSpirituality.org,* for more spiritual resources, and follow us on Facebook for regular updates: *facebook.com/RCSpirituality.*

If you would like to support and sponsor a Retreat Guide, please consider making a donation at RCSpirituality.org.

Retreat Guides are a service of Regnum Christi.
RegnumChristi.org

Produced by Coronation Media.
CoronationMedia.com

Developed & Self-published by RCSpirituality.
RCSpirituality.org

www.ingramcontent.com/pod-product-compliance
Lightning Source LLC
Chambersburg PA
CBHW051401150726

48000CB00003B/1281